DSM-5
MIS*UNDERSTOOD*

An overview to understanding Disorders

Maria Shkreli, LMHC

This guide contains summarized information relating to mental health. It is not intended to replace medical advice and should not be used to supplement mental health care. The information provided is a summarization and comparison of similarities of disorders, treatments, and assessment practices, to be used as a quick reference guide for individuals studying in the mental health field. All efforts have been made to ensure the accuracy of the information provided. Both publisher and author disclaim any liability for any methods applied or suggested in this guide.

First edition: March 2020

Printed in the United States of America.

ISBN-13: 978-0-578-66018-9

To my kids Christopher & Nicolette

Always reach for the stars!
Believe in you!

Contents

Italicized, bold, and colored words and sentences are used to point out the differences and/or the similarities in symptoms.

Contents

Italicized, bold, and colored words and sentences are used to point out the differences and/or the similarities in symptoms.

Contents

Italicized, bold, and colored words and sentences are used to point out the differences and/or the similarities in symptoms.

Congratulations on purchasing your new study guide. My goal in writing this guide is to cover and compare the differences and similarities between various DSM-5 disorders in a simplified format. *The study guide is a supplement to be used with other study materials purchased.*

Many times, people focus on memorizing and don't pay attention to learning the information needed to understand disorders. Too often, information overload confuses an individual, and the result is not understanding or not learning the information. This, in turn, causes anxiety and fears that create doubt about the material you thought you knew.

This guide is designed to be simple and to the point in order to increase your knowledge and understanding of the material needed to know pertaining to diagnosis.

Remember, this guide is not the full DSM-5 criteria. It contains brief references of disorders and theoretical orientations in a format intended to help you recognize similarities and differences, test your knowledge, and use a quick reference.

Thank you for your purchase, and the best of luck to you in your career path.

Sincerely,

Maria Shkreli, LMHC

DSM-5 MisUnderstood

Introduction

Leaning the DSM-5 is not about memorizing terms its about understanding the disorder so a clinician can diagnosis patients. The DSM-5 is used by clinicians, psychiatrists, therapist, counselors and students.

The original version was published in 1994, and listed more than 250 mental disorders. In 2013, the latest version was published the DSM-5. Changes to the DSM-5 contain significant changes that include:

- Shift of using Arabic numbers
- Eliminated the axis system
- Listing categories of disorders
- Several diagnosis were added, binge eating disorder, hoarding disorder, and premenstrual dysphonic disorder
- Asperger's is incorporated under the autism spectrum disorders

The purpose of this guide is to be used as a reference and tool to help those learning about disorders. Why did I did to write this guide, because through my own experience, I found that keeping it simple made the difference in understanding and learning. Since we are all different learners, finding ways to gain insight into learning material can be stressful and overwhelming. I discovered that the many guides I purchased contained too much information scattered throughout the book; they listed the disorders and theoretical orientations but did not explain how they varied and worked together, which made them a challenge.

I have written this guide in a format for individuals to learn the material and not just to memorize a disorder. I hope you find it useful and please feel free to email me at mgshkreli@gmail.com with any questions and/or comments.

What you will find in this guide:

A Brief description of specific DSM-5 disorders.

A Brief description of theoretical orientation used in therapy.

How to breakdown a disorder.

Maria

Professionals use the DSM-5 as reference for diagnosis. Professionals also rely on patient self-report, observing presenting symptoms of their patients and asses them using the DSM-5 to diagnosis. Once a diagnosis is determined a clinician will proceed with a treatment plan for their patient.

The DSM-5 is to only be used by trained professionals as a diagnosis tool in treating psychological disorders and it is not recommended to be used by untrained professionals.

To better help your understanding of disorders In the next few chapters, you will find summarized disorders so you can better learn the disorders, similarities and differences between disorders.

Chapter 2

Anxiety Disorders

Agoraphobia
Generalized Anxiety Disorder
Panic Disorder
Selective Mutism
Separation Anxiety Disorder
Social Anxiety Disorder

Anxiety Disorders

Disorder	Overview
Panic Disorder *Experiences* **PHYSICAL SENSATION*	**The individual experiences uncontrollable, recurrent episodes of panic and fear within minutes and is preoccupied with the fear of a recurring attack.** The individual must experience persistent concern about having a panic attack. In addition, the individual may have developed avoidance behaviors to prevent triggers. **At least 1 month. Sudden & intense PANIC** Four of the following symptoms must occur during a panic attack: 1. Pounding heart 2. Shortness of breath 3. Chest discomfort 4. Nausea 5. Dizziness, lightheadedness 6. Fear of losing control 7. Fear of dying 8. Numbness 9. Chills or hot flashes 10. Sweating 11. Choking feeling 12. Trembling 13. Feeling detached from reality
Generalized Anxiety Disorder *Experiences* **PHYSICAL SYMPTOM*	**The individual has excessive worry about events or activities, such as money, family, or work. EXCESSIVE worry** **This anxiety must exist for at least six months** and must be difficult to control. The anxiety is also disproportionate to the fear. Anxiety must include three of the following: 1. Sleep disturbance 2. Irritability 3. Difficulty concentrating 4. Muscle tension 5. Exertion or fatigue 6. Restlessness 7. Chronic headaches

Anxiety Disorders

Disorder	Overview
Separation Anxiety Disorder	**The individual experiences excessive anxiety when separated from an individual to whom they are attached.** The child must have symptoms that last for **at least four weeks and the onset must occur before the age of 18.** Individual will manifest the following symptoms: 1. Extreme distress when separated from home or the attachment figure 2. Persistent fear of being alone 3. Frequent physical complaints while separated from the attachment figure
Social Anxiety Disorder	**Persistent fear of social situations or a situation when the individual may need to perform.** The fear/anxiety has a negative impact on the individual's life and **must be present for at least six months.** Individual will experience distress in the following situations: 1. Meeting other people 2. Easily embarrassed 3. Feeling insecure and out of place 4. Having to speak in public 5. Being the center of attention 6. Being criticized
Agoraphobia	**The individual is anxious about being outside of the home or in open places.** **Fear of a PANIC ATTACK occurring when leaving the home, not a fear of people.** Symptoms are **present for at least six months:** 1. Fear of being outside the home 2. Fear of public transportation 3. Fear of enclosed/open places 4. Fear of inability to escape when needed
Selective Mutism	**A complex childhood anxiety disorder characterized by a child's inability to speak in a social setting when it's appropriate to speak.** Symptoms are **present for at least one month:** 1. Doesn't speak when he/she should 2. Lack of speaking gets in the way of school and friendships 3. Doesn't have a speech problem

Chapter 3

Stressor-Related and Trauma Disorders

Acute Stress Disorder
Adjustment Disorder
Disinhibited Social Engagement Disorder
Posttraumatic Stress Disorder
Reactive Attachment Disorder

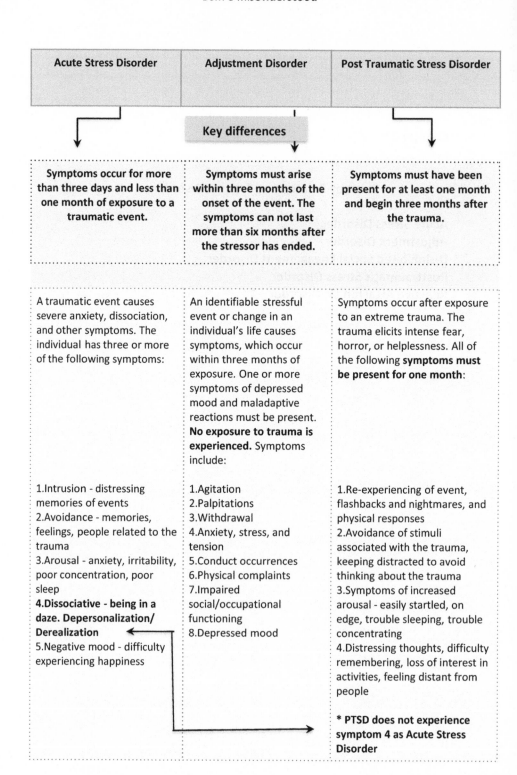

Acute Stress Disorder	Adjustment Disorder	Post Traumatic Stress Disorder

Key differences

Symptoms occur for more than three days and less than one month of exposure to a traumatic event.	Symptoms must arise within three months of the onset of the event. The symptoms can not last more than six months after the stressor has ended.	Symptoms must have been present for at least one month and begin three months after the trauma.
A traumatic event causes severe anxiety, dissociation, and other symptoms. The individual has three or more of the following symptoms:	An identifiable stressful event or change in an individual's life causes symptoms, which occur within three months of exposure. One or more symptoms of depressed mood and maladaptive reactions must be present. **No exposure to trauma is experienced.** Symptoms include:	Symptoms occur after exposure to an extreme trauma. The trauma elicits intense fear, horror, or helplessness. All of the following **symptoms must be present for one month**:
1.Intrusion - distressing memories of events 2.Avoidance - memories, feelings, people related to the trauma 3.Arousal - anxiety, irritability, poor concentration, poor sleep **4.Dissociative - being in a daze. Depersonalization/ Derealization** ← 5.Negative mood - difficulty experiencing happiness	1.Agitation 2.Palpitations 3.Withdrawal 4.Anxiety, stress, and tension 5.Conduct occurrences 6.Physical complaints 7.Impaired social/occupational functioning 8.Depressed mood	1.Re-experiencing of event, flashbacks and nightmares, and physical responses 2.Avoidance of stimuli associated with the trauma, keeping distracted to avoid thinking about the trauma 3.Symptoms of increased arousal - easily startled, on edge, trouble sleeping, trouble concentrating 4.Distressing thoughts, difficulty remembering, loss of interest in activities, feeling distant from people *** PTSD does not experience symptom 4 as Acute Stress Disorder**

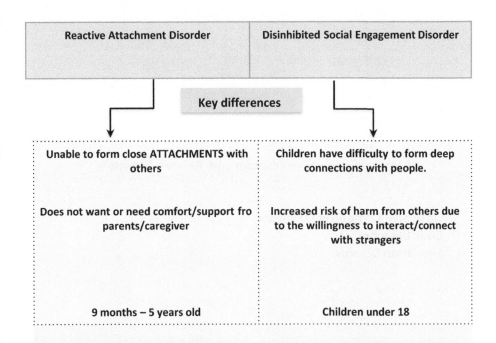

Reactive Attachment Disorder	Disinhibited Social Engagement Disorder

Key differences

Unable to form close ATTACHMENTS with others	Children have difficulty to form deep connections with people.
Does not want or need comfort/support fro parents/caregiver	Increased risk of harm from others due to the willingness to interact/connect with strangers
9 months – 5 years old	**Children under 18**

An attachment disorder is when a child is unable to establish healthy attachment with parents or their caregiver. The child feels alone and unsafe. The child has been subjected to abuse or neglect and failed to establish a bond.	An attachment disorder is when a child lacks appropriate affection and nurturing from parents. Because of this the child is not bonded with parents and will be comfortable with strangers. The child's caregiving environment may have consisted of, abandonment, orphanage, foster case, or suffered trauma or severe contentious emotional and social neglect.
Symptoms include:	**Symptoms include:**
1.Failure to smile, withdrawn when parent of caregiver attempt to interact with them 2.Don't respond to the movement of the parent or caregiver, not interested in what going on, including playing games 3.The self soothe themselves 4.When in distress they calm themselves, without the attention of a parent/caregiver	1.No shyness of meeting people or fear of adult strangers 2.Overfriendly or talkative to strangers 3.Does not seek permission for parents to approach strangers 4.Not fearful of leaving with strangers 5.Physical with strangers, hugging/cuddling **Symptoms may continue into adulthood**

Chapter 4

Obsessive Compulsive Disorder and Related Disorders

Obsessive Compulsive Disorder
Body Dysmoprhic
Exoriation Disorder

Obsessive Compulsive Disorder and Related Disorders

Disorder	Overview
Obsessive Compulsive Disorder	OCD is an ANXIETY disorder. Presence of true OBSESSION and/or COMPULSION. It is characterized by an individual's disturbing thoughts of obsessions or compulsions (some individuals may have both) that impact their daily lives. Some individuals may spend an hour a day on these behaviors. **Obsessions include:** •Continuous, persistent thoughts that cause distress. Attempts to ignore the thoughts, urges, images, and causes that lead to the compulsive behavior •Unfounded suspicion of individuals •Need for orderliness •Need for cleanliness; fear of germs **Compulsions:** •Repetitive behaviors in which the individual feels inclined to perform in response to an obsession •Repetitive behaviors include: washing of hands, performing certain tasks a certain number of times, checking appliances a certain number of times •Behavioral acts are aimed at reducing anxiety or distress or preventing a feared event
Body Dysmorphic Disorder * **The symptoms that must meet criteria for diagnosis are bolded**	An individual is preoccupied with perceived flaws in various areas of the body. **Attention to at least once perceived flaw in physical appearance**. Individual will engage in repetitive behaviors in receiving reassurance about their appearance. This condition has to do with an individuals how they see themselves. **Most often develops in adolescents and teens.** Symptoms may include: •**Compares body parts to others appearance** •Seeks surgery to correct perceived flaw •**Constantly checks in a mirror** •Avoids mirrors •Excessive grooming •Excessive exercise routines •Excessively changes clothing •Camouflages with, hair, clothing, make-up •**Preoccupation that causes distress, unable to function effectively in life** •**Concern can not relate to an eating disorder**

Obsessive Compulsive Disorder and Related Disorders

Disorder	Overview
Excoriation Disorder (Know as skin picking.)	Skin-picking disorder is a repetitive grooming behavior. The picking is chronic and individuals pick their skin out of habit or impulse. It is a recurrent behavior that results in noticeable scares, scabs and sores. **Symptoms include:** •Attempting to remove imperfections •Spending a lot of time picking – an individual with spend several times and/or hours a day picking their skin •Developing scars and/or infection from the skin picking. •Avoiding public events because of the lesions and scars on the skin, e.g... The beach, a party usually when revealing clothing is worn **•This disorder is common co-occurring with the following:** Obsessive Compulsive Disorder Body Dysmorphic disorder Major Depressive Disorder Trichotillomania (hair pulling)

Chapter 5

Bipolar and related disorders

Bipolar I
Bipolar II
Cyclothymic Disorder

Bipolar and Related Disorders

Disorder	Overview
Bipolar I (also known as manic depressive) • **MUST have a manic episode** • CAN have a hypomanic episode • Can have a depressive episode	A disorder characterized by episodes of elevated mood, with alternating episodes of depression. Significantly elevated mood. **Symptoms persistent for most of the day and last at least one week (or less, if hospitalized).** • Excessive talking • Less need for sleep • Poor appetite, weight loss • Aggressive behavior • Easily distracted • Flight of ideas • Inflated self-esteem • Engages in activities that can have negative consequences
Bipolar II • Never has a manic episode • **MUST have a hypomanic episode (lasts for four days)** • **MUST have a depressive episode**	A disorder characterized by a pattern of one or more major depressive episodes and at least one hypomanic episode. Depressive episode never severe enough to cause impairment in functioning, or to require hospitalization. **Symptoms last four days.** • Inflated self-esteem • Less need for sleep • Very talkative • Racing thoughts • Excessive talking • Engages in activities that can have negative consequences

KEY DIFFERENCES

Bipolar I: Mania is more severe; Bipolar II: Experiences hypomania

Bipolar and Related Disorders

Disorder	Overview
Cyclothymic Disorder	The individual's symptoms alternate between highs and lows of hypomanic and depressive (mild form) and are chronic. Hypomania/depression are **present for at least half the time and not more than two consecutive months without symptoms over a two-year period** (one for children). **Symptoms are present for two years in adults, and for at least one year in children/adolescents.** **Depressive symptoms (symptoms can never meet criteria for a major depressive episode):** •Sadness/hopelessness •Irritability •Low self-esteem •Loss of interest in activities •Inability to concentrate •Loneliness •Social withdrawal **Hypomanic symptoms (symptoms can never meet criteria for a hypomanic episode):** •Irritable •Easily distracted •Increased drive •Overeating •Impulsive •More talkative •Racing thoughts

Chapter 6

Depressive Disorders

Disruptive Mood Dysregulation Disorder
Major Depressive Disorder
Persistent Depressive Disorder
Postpartum Depression
Seasonal Affective Disorder

Depressive Disorders

Disorder	Overview
Major Depressive Disorder (in adults)	**A serious mood disorder. Severe symptoms that affect daily activities, how one thinks, how one feels, eating habits, and sleep habits. The mood of intense sadness is for an extended period of time.** **An individual experiences five or more of the following symptoms for two consecutive weeks:** •Loss of interest in activities and/or ability to feel pleasure •Depressed mood •Decrease or increase in appetite (weight gain or loss) •Insomnia (often) or hypersomnia (sleeps excessively) •Feelings of worthlessness/guilt •Loss of energy; fatigue •Thoughts of death •Motor agitation - poor memory and concentration **Episodes cause distress and/or social impairment. Episodes do not meet criteria for substance abuse, manic episode, hypomanic episode, schizophrenia, or other psychotic disorders.**
Major Depressive disorder (in children)	**Young children will be depressed and/or irritable most of the time. They also lose interest in activities (most of the time) for at least two weeks:** •Crankiness and/or irritability •Unusual sadness •Reduced interest in activities, friends •No longer sees things as pleasurable •Changes in weight •Changes in sleep patterns; sluggishness •Inappropriate guilt, harsh on themselves •Extreme case, kids have thoughts of or make attempt at suicide

Depressive Disorders

Disorder	Overview
Persistent Depressive Disorder (formerly known as Dysthymic)	This disorder shares symptoms with major depressive and dysthymic disorder. The symptoms are less severe but chronic. The feelings of sadness and hopelessness are continuous. **Depressive symptoms are present for two years and for most of each day. Symptoms must be present for at least one year for adolescents and children.** **Two or more of the following:** •Low self-esteem •Decreased appetite or overeating •Feeling of hopelessness •Fatigue •Unable to concentrate •Insomnia •Anger/irritability •Sadness •Difficulty concentrating •Decrease in productivity **Episodes do not meet criteria for major depressive disorder, cyclothymic disorder, manic episode, schizophrenia, or other psychotic disorders.**
Disruptive Mood Dysregulation Disorder (Children - Teenagers)	This disorder involves persistent, irritable, or angry moods and frequent temper outbursts that are disproportionate to the situation. Similar to ODD and Bipolar. **Diagnosis is new, therefore effective therapy treatment is in new stages of effectiveness.** **Symptoms must be present before the age of 10 and not after the age of 18. Diagnosis is not to be made before the age of six.** **Symptoms must be present for 12 months:** •Often irritable or angry for most of the day •Frequent severe temper outbursts that are out of proportion to the situation occur an average of three times a week •Temper is inconsistent •The temper outbursts are present at home and in school

Depressive Disorders

Disorder	Overview
Postpartum Depression (specifier within Major Depressive Disorder)	A form of depression experienced by women after childbirth. Symptoms can start within the first few weeks of childbirth or months after childbirth. Depressive symptoms, sadness, can interfere with a woman's ability to care for her family and herself. The likelihood of experiencing postpartum depression is higher for women with a history of depression. **Common symptoms include:** •Frequent crying •Irritability or anxiety •Loss of interest or pleasure in activities •Loss of appetite •Low motivation and energy •Little interest in the baby •Weight loss or gain •Hopelessness, guilty feeling •Disruption of sleep, too much sleep, not enough sleep
Seasonal Affective Disorder (specifier within Major Depressive Disorder)	A form of depression that occurs at the same time every year. Most common in the fall and early winter and lasting until the spring or summer. An individual must meet the criteria for major depression coinciding with specific seasons. **Symptoms must be present for two years** **Winter symptoms include:** •Possible weight gain •Desire to be alone •Increase in appetite •Difficulty in concentrating •Headaches •Irritable and anxious •Loss of energy and/or fatigue **Summer symptoms include:** •Decrease in appetite •Sleep disturbances •Change in appetite or weight •Insomnia •Irritability and anxiety

Chapter 7

Personality Disorders

Antisocial Personality Disorder
Avoidant Personality Disorder
Borderline Personality Disorder
Conversion Disorder
Dependent Personality Disorder
Factitious Disorder
Histrionic Personality Disorder
Malingering Disorder
Narcissistic Personality Disorder
Obsessive Compulsive Personality Disorder
Paranoid Personality Disorder
Schizoid Personality Disorder
Schizotypal Personality Disorder
Somatic Symptom Disorder

Personality Disorders

Disorder	Overview
Borderline Personality Disorder	**Is a mental condition that begins in adolescence or early adulthood. includes impulsive behavior and reckless behavior, unstable relationships and moods. Individual suffer BRIEF PSYCHOTIC mood swings.** Individual displays a pervasive pattern of instability in affect, impulsivity, instability of social relationships, and self-image. Tend to have "all-or-nothing" thinking. Requires five of the following symptoms: 1.Inappropriate behavior 2.Constant feelings of emptiness 3.Affective instability 4.Recurring suicide threats **5.Self-destructive impulsivity in at least two areas** 6.Paranoid ideation/dissociative symptoms 7.Unstable self-image 8.Patterns of unstable and intense personal relationships (idealization and devaluation) 9.Fear of being abandoned
Histrionic Personality Disorder	**Individual is vulnerable (emotionally) and needs constant praise from people. Inappropriately seductive, manipulative, and flirtatious.** Individual is excessively emotional and exhibits attention-seeking behavior. Requires five of the following symptoms: **1.Physical appearance to draw attention** 2.Believes relationships are intimate when they are not 3.Easily influenced by individuals 4.Exaggerated expression of emotion 5.Impressionistic speech 6.Shifting and shallow emotion 7.Inappropriate sexual provocation 8.Discomfort when not receiving attention needed

Personality Disorders

Disorder	Overview
Narcissistic Personality Disorder **Individual has a significantly inflated sense of self-worth. Lacks empathy, has an arrogant attitude, is envious, and exploits other individuals.**	Individual has an extreme preoccupation with self; their distorted thoughts give them a sense of extreme confidence. They tend to have low self-esteem and are generally disappointed when they are not admired. Requires five or more of the following symptoms: 1.Grandiose sense of self 2.Occupied with fantasies; includes level of power they have, success, brilliance 3.They feel they are unique 4.They require admiration 5.They have a sense of strong entitlement 6.They are arrogant and conceited 7.Monopolize conversations and look down on others 8.Expect to be seen as superior and feel they can only be around other superior people 9.Take advantage of others When these individuals feel criticized, they may react in the following manner: *Angry and/or depressed when they don't receive the attention they feel they deserve *Belittle others to make themselves feel superior
Avoidant Personality Disorder ***LACK of SOCIAL INTEREST & inadequacy due to fear of criticism.**	Individuals are characterized by patterns of feeling inadequate, socially inhibited, and hypersensitivity. Feelings also involve anxiety or fearfulness. **Four of these symptoms must be present:** •Fear of excelling in new situations – feels inadequate •Avoids activities that involve interpersonal contact •Sees self as unappealing, inferior, or socially incompetent •Reluctant to take risks or engage in threatening behavior •Preoccupied with being criticized or rejected •Fear of being shamed in an intimate relationships •Unwilling to interact with people who may not approve of them •Fearful and tense demeanor •Lack of trust in others

Personality Disorders

Disorder	Overview
Paranoid Personality Disorder **IRRATIONAL FEAR or PARANOIA that someone intends to harm them**	**The individual displays a continuous pattern of suspicion of others and is difficult to get along with. The individual assumes that personal and professional relationships have malignant motives towards them.** Individual must have had at least four or more of the following symptoms: 1.Fear or anxiety is out of proportion to the actual threat 2.Doubts the trustworthiness of others 3.Hesitant to confide in others 4.Suspicions of a partner's fidelity without justification 5.Reads hidden meanings into remarks 6.Maintains constant grudges 7.Believes attacks on his/her character by others 8.Believes in conspiracy theories 9.Constantly feels threatened by loved ones and/or stranger
Antisocial Personality Disorder	**The individual displays patterns of manipulation and violation of other individuals. Patterns begin during childhood or early adolescence and continue into adulthood. Emotional, erratic, and dramatic behaviors. A lack of concern toward the rights and feelings of others** The following criteria must be met: •**Must be at least 18** •**History of conduct disorder before age of 15** •**Has shown at least 3 of the following symptoms before the age of 15:** •Irritability/aggression •Deceitfulness •Impulsivity •Reckless disregard for the safety of self and others •Lack of remorse •Failure to conform to social norms and laws •Consistent irresponsibility

Personality Disorders

Disorder	Overview
Malingering Disorder	Physical symptoms to avoid a specific activity, such as going to work or receiving an award: 1.Individual obtains medical evaluation for legal reasons and may also apply for insurance compensation 2.Individual has a marked inconsistency between the complaint and the findings Individual does not cooperate with diagnostic evaluation or treatment 3.Individual has an antisocial personality disorder 4.Voluntary
Factitious Disorder	An individual intentionally manifests physical or psychological symptoms in order to satisfy the need to fill the role of a sick person: 1.Presents an illness in an exaggerated manner 2.Avoids questioning from others that may expose the truth 3.May undergo multiple surgeries 4.May undergo medical procedures 5.May hide insurance claim forms from others 6.Voluntary
Somatic Symptom Disorder	Individual may suggest a medical condition exists but isn't explainable: 1.Symptoms are dramatic and overstated 2.Worries extensively about the symptoms. Spends a lot of time worrying about health issues 3.Worrying causes distress 4.Recurrent complaints (a symptom may be present for six months) 5.No medical explanation has been found
Conversion Disorder	The loss of bodily function; or serious physical disease: 1.Individual may become blind, mute, or paralyzed due to an acute stressor 2.Vomiting, coughing spells, or hyperesthesia may develop 3.The symptoms tested do not reveal underlying disease 4.Sensory loss, movement loss, or repetition of movements that are not intentional 5.May be used to maintain internal conflict 6.May be used by a person to avoid an activity 7.Not voluntary

Personality Disorders

Disorder	Overview
Obsessive Compulsive Personality Disorder	**OCPD is STRICT ADHERENCE to orderliness and control over one's environment at the expense of flexibility to new experiences.** **Characterized by strict adherence to orderliness and control. The control over their environment makes the individual inflexible and not open to new experiences.** **Symptoms include:** •Preoccupation with details, rules, and organization that affect the job at hand and make one inefficient •Perfectionism that interferes with daily tasks at work, school, or home •Excessive devotion to the productivity of a job, which jeopardizes social life •Is overly diligent about values and morals •Has a difficult time discarding old objects and materials that provide no use •Tendency to have black and white thinking and stubbornness •Hesitant to work with others •When working with others, the need for control is prevalent •Difficulty expressing emotions and feelings, affects relationships • Has difficulty maintaining relationships
Dependent Personality Disorder	**Persistent dependence on other people - manifests itself by early adulthood.** Individual will manifest the following symptoms: 1. The need to be taken care of 2. Inability to make decisions on their own 3. Relies on others to assume responsibility for their life 4. Relies on the constant advice of others 5. Difficulties with expressing disagreements 6. Fear of separation 7. Feeling of helplessness

Personality Disorders

Disorder	Overview
Schizotypal Personality Disorder **AVOIDS social interaction due to fear of people.**	Individuals with this disorder have difficulties forming and maintaining relationships. The individuals are characterized by pervasive social deficits, behavior oddities of cognition, inappropriate social cues, and misinterpretation of people's motivations. **Five of these symptoms must be present:** •Excessive social anxiety •Ideas of reference •Odd beliefs/magical thinking •Lacks close friends (excluding family) •Bodily illusions •Suspiciousness/paranoid ideation •Inappropriate /constricted affect •Peculiarities in appearance or behavior
Schizoid Personality Disorder **FEELS NO DESIRE to form relationships, doesn't see the point, enjoys solitary lifestyle.**	Individuals are characterized by lack of interest in relationships with others, and limited emotional expression with others (coldness, detachment, or flattened affectivity). **Four of these symptoms must be present:** •Lacks close friends (excluding family) •Detachment or emotional coldness •Takes pleasure in few activities •Little interest in sexual relationships •Almost always chooses solitary activities •Indifferent to praise/criticism

Chapter 8
___

Schizophrenia and other Psychotic Disorder

Brief Psychotic Disorder
Delusional Disorder
Schizoaffective Disorder
Schizophrenia Disorder
Schizophreniform Disorder
Schizotypal Personality Disorder

Schizophrenia and other Psychotic Disorders

Disorder	Overview
Schizoaffective **Schizoaffective symptoms overlap with bipolar, depressive disorder, and schizophrenia.	An individual who experiences persistent psychotic symptoms (schizophrenia symptoms) and major mood disorder (depression or bipolar disorder). **Symptoms are present for at least two weeks and have to be present for most of the time and meet the criteria for a major mood disorder. The amount of time an individual experiences severe mood symptoms accounts for more than half of the total duration of the illness.** Two primary types are: •**Bipolar type** requires at least one manic episode •**Depressive type** requires only major depressive episodes **Symptoms include the following:** •Delusions •Hallucinations •Disorganized speech •Grossly disorganized/ catatonic behavior •Negative symptoms **Bipolar type:** •Episodes of mania & sometimes major depression (see bipolar definition) **Depressive type:** •Depressed mood •Inability to sleep •Lack of energy •Feeling of guilt •Difficulty in concentration •Change in weight •Lack of pleasure in activities

Schizophrenia and other Psychotic Disorders

Disorder	Overview
Schizophrenia	An individual who experiences psychosis (cannot tell the difference between real and imagined) is unable to express emotion or relate to others. **Acute symptoms must be present for one month and continuous signs of symptoms present for at least six months. Symptoms are described as either positive or negative.** Must present two or more symptoms: **Positive Symptoms:** •Delusions •Hallucinations •Grossly disorganized/ catatonic behavior/ thinking/speech •Disorganized behavior - lack of proper hygiene, choosing the appropriate clothing for the weather, impulsive actions **Negative symptoms:** •Flat affect •Lack of pleasure in life •Inability to start/ continue productive activities •Limited ability to engage in conversation with others •Lack of motivation •Withdrawal from social activities, friends and family **Cognitive symptoms:** •Poor executive functioning •Working memory •Trouble focusing

Schizophrenia and other Psychotic Disorders

Disorder	Overview
Brief Psychotic Disorder	The individual experiences psychotic symptoms due to extreme trauma, stress, assault, or death of a loved one. **Symptoms are present for at least one day and less than one month.** • Delusions • Hallucinations • Disorganized speech • Grossly disorganized/catatonic behavior
Schizophreniform **Symptoms are similar to schizophrenia, but duration of symptoms sets the diagnosis for Schizophreniform.**	An individual who experiences psychosis (cannot tell the difference between real and imagined) for at least one month but less than six months. This disorder is on the schizophrenia spectrum and needs two major symptoms for diagnosis. **Symptoms last for at least one month but less than six months.** Must present two symptoms (one must be either 1, 2, or 3): Delusions 2. Hallucinations 3. Disorganized speech •Abnormal body movements, repeating motions over and over •Negative symptoms

Schizophrenia and other Psychotic Disorders

Disorder	Overview
Schizotypal Personality Disorder **AVOIDS social interaction due to fear of people.**	Individuals with this disorder have difficulties forming and maintaining relationships. The individuals are characterized by pervasive social deficits, behavior oddities of cognition, inappropriate social cues, and misinterpretation of people's motivations. **Five of these symptoms must be present:** •Excessive social anxiety •Ideas of reference •Odd beliefs/magical thinking •Lacks close friends (excluding family) •Bodily illusions •Suspiciousness/paranoid ideation •Inappropriate /constricted affect •Peculiarities in appearance or behavior
Delusional Disorder	**The individual is characterized by either bizarre or non-bizarre presence of delusions for at least one month or longer. The individual does not meet the criteria for schizophrenia.** Aside from the delusions, the individual's functioning is not impaired, and behavior is not bizarre or odd enough to affect daily functioning. **The following are different types of delusions:** **Erotomanic:** The individual believes that an important person (famous person) is in love with them. **Grandiose:** The individual has an over-inflated sense of self. Presence of persistent delusion. **Jealous type:** The individual continuously believes that his or her partner or spouse is unfaithful to the relationship. **Persecutory:** The individual believes they are being spied on and others are out to get them. **Somatic type:** The individual believes they have a medical issue or physical defects. **Mixed types:** The individual has two or more of the delusions listed above.

Chapter 9

Dissociative Disorders

Depersonalization/Derealization Disorder
Dissociative Amnesia
Dissociative Identity Disorder

Dissociative Disorders

Dissociative Disorders are frequently associated with previous trauma in an individual's life. Symptoms involve disturbances of mental functioning.

Disorder	Overview
Dissociative Identity Disorder (formerly Multiple Personality Disorder)	**When two or more personalities (identity fragments) exist within a person's identity. Individuals with this disorder are often victims of severe abuse.** **Symptoms:** •The personalities are dominant at particular times/ situations. Each personality has its own sense of self •The identity is a change in behavior and consciousness, cognition, and perception •Memory loss; includes not remembering people, places, events, or personal information •Sense of detachment from self, causing distress or impairment in social occupation function and other areas of functioning
Dissociative Amnesia	**The inability to recall important personal information about self, not to be confused with normal forgetfulness.** **Variations include:** **Localized** •The inability to recall an event or a period of time **Selective** •The inability to recall a specific event or period of time **Generalized** •The inability to recall one's own life history
Depersonalization/ Derealization Disorder	**When an individual feels detached from themselves; looking into self from the outside. Individual is aware of how they feel and see the world, but can't explain why this is happening.** **Depersonalization** •The individual can feel detached, as if they are outside their bodies. The individual feels they are watching events from the outside - not being in the now. **Derealization** •The individual feels that things, events, and people aren't real

Chapter 10

Conduct and Disruptive Disorders

Conduct Disorder
Intermittent Explosive Disorder
Kleptomania
Oppositional Defiant Disorder
Pyromania

Conduct and Disruptive Disorders

Disorder	Overview
Oppositional Defiant Disorder Children (age 3-18)	Patterns of argumentative behavior and attitudes toward authority figures. **Key Characteristic: Fighting Against Being Controlled** **Symptoms must disrupt their school, social, and home life and be present for at least six months.** **Children under 5: The behaviors occur on most days for at least six months.** For some children, symptoms may only show in one environment - home. **Category I (often)** •Easily loses temper •Frequently touchy or easily annoyed •Angry or resentful **Category II (often)** •Argues with adults and/or authority figures •Actively defies and/or refuses to comply with rules and requests from authority figures •Deliberately annoys others •Blames others for their mistakes or misbehavior **Category III** •Often vindictive or spiteful •Has been spiteful or vindictive at least twice within the past six months

Conduct and Disruptive Disorders

Disorder	Overview
Conduct Disorder Appears before age 10 - by age 16	Serious emotional and behavioral problems in adolescents and children. **Key Characteristic: Will Attempt To Control Others** **Symptoms commonly begin by the age of 16**. At least three of these behaviors must have occurred within the past year with one occurring within the past six months. **Category I** Aggressive behaviors toward people and animals, including bullying, intimidating people, physical violence, forced sexual acts, weapon use, or inflicting physical cruelty to people or animals. **Category II** Has deliberately engaged in property destruction or setting fires. **Category III** •Has broken into someone's home, building, or car and stolen something •Often lies to gain goods or favors or to avoid obligations **Category IV** •Often stays out late at night, despite parental rules (before age of 13) •Has run away from home overnight at least twice without returning for a long period of time •Is often truant from school (before the age of 13)

Conduct and Disruptive Disorders

Disorder	Overview
Intermittent Explosive Disorder (Late Childhood - Adolescence)	This disorder involves repeated, sudden episodes of impulsive, aggressive, and/ or angry verbal outbursts, in which the individual reacts disproportionately to the situation. **Symptoms occur suddenly, with no warning, and usually last less than 30 minutes.** **Aggressive:** •Verbal aggression •Rage •Irritability •Increased energy **The outbursts can include:** •Temper tantrums •Elevated arguments •Tirades •Shouting •Slapping or shoving •Destruction or damage of property and/or physical assault involving physical injury against individuals or animals

Conduct and Disruptive Disorders

Disorder	Overview
Pyromania	A pathological disorder by intentionally setting repeated fires. Feels of satisfaction for the individual **Symptoms:** •Attraction to fire •Purposely setting more than one fire •Feeling of excitement, tense before fire setting and relief after the fire is et •No monetary gain for the fire setting •Not explained by a manic episode
Kleptomania	Is an act of taking something that doesn't belong to you without permission. This is considered a psychological compulsion because the individual seeks no reward for the act. The individual has urges to steal things they don't need. Items can usually be afforded by the individual. The strong urges prior to the theft leave the Individual satisfied once the act is committed. Individuals will feel remorse after the act is over. **Symptoms:** •Repeated inability to resist the urges to steal •The act ends in a feeling of gratification, relief •Not for personal gain

Chapter 11

Neurodevelopmental Disorders

Attention Deficit/Hyperactivity Disorder
Autism Spectrum Disorder
Communication Disorder
Intellectual Disability
Learning Disorders
Motor Disorders

Neurodevelopmental Disorders

Disorder	Overview
Attention Deficit/Hyperactivity Disorder (ADHD)	**Difficult to concentrate, pay attention, sit still, and/or limit impulsivity.** May be eligible for IEP "Other Health Component" – Accommodations can be provided under a 504 plan. **Must present at least six symptoms of inattention AND/OR hyperactivity-impulsivity.** **Onset before the age of 12 and persists for at least six months.** **Inattentive type** •Frequently loses items •Forgetfulness •Easily distracted by extraneous stimuli •Fails to complete chores or schoolwork •Difficulty sustaining participation in activities and tasks •Difficulty listening when addressed •Avoids tasks that require focus **Hyperactive-impulsive type** •Intrudes on others' space/time •Difficulty playing quietly •Running in inappropriate settings •Fidgeting or squirming in a seat/looks to get out of seat •Excessive talking •Always seems restless •Interrupts often

Neurodevelopmental Disorders

Disorder	Overview
Autism Spectrum Disorder (ASD)	**Neurodevelopmental condition that causes challenges with social skills, communication, and thinking – repetitive behavior is part of diagnosis.** **May be eligible for IEP "Autism." Special Education may be provided with accommodations.** Two categories for diagnosis of autism spectrum disorder: **Impairment in social interactions and in communication:** •Poor eye contact •Delayed speech or loss of speech •Lack of ability to express emotions or feelings •Inappropriate social interaction; disruptive, aggressive •Lack of ability to sustain or initiate conversation •Speaks with abnormal rhythm •Lack of developmentally appropriate play •Absence of developmentally appropriate relationships (peer) •Lack of ability to recognize nonverbal cues, such as interpreting other people's facial expressions, body language **Behavior patterns may include:** •Performs repetitive movements, such as hand flapping •Has difficulty with coordination, such as clumsiness or walking on toes •Has fascination with detail of objects, but doesn't understand the function of the object, such as the wheel on a toy car •Has high abnormal focus •Has specific food preferences •Has specific routines and/or rituals **Noticeable specific behavior patterns:** **Lack of eye contact - disinterest in others – rarely reaches out to others – repeating the words of others – obsessive interest in narrow subjects – extreme emphasis on routine and consistency.**

Neurodevelopmental Disorders

Disorder	Overview
Intellectual Disorder	Intellectual involves cognitive limitations, skills, communication, social skills and self-care skills of an individual. Intellectual disability meets the following: •IQ below 70-75 •Limitations in adaptive areas; work, social skills, communication, self-care •Condition happens before the age of 18
Communication Disorders	Disorders that affect the ability to apply language and speech with other individuals. **Symptoms:** Speech disorder – difficulty in making speech sounds. Fluency disorder (stuttering) – begins between the ages of two and seven. Speech is repetitive, has hesitations or disturbance in flow. Language disorder – has difficulty in relaying their meaning to others using speech.
Learning Disorders	Interferes with an individual's ability to learn basic skills: reading, writing, and math. Common disabilities include: •Dyslexia •ADHD •Dysgraphia •Dyscalculia •Processing defects **Symptoms:** Spelling incorrectly Difficulty with syntax and grammar Difficulty reading Difficulty with understanding what is read Difficulty with math calculation Difficulty with math reasoning

Neurodevelopmental Disorders

Disorder	Overview
Motor Disorders	Involves coordination disorders, stereotypic movement disorder, and tic disorder (formerly Tourette's Disorder). **Coordination Disorder** •Clumsiness •Delayed sitting, walking, and crawling •Difficulty with jumping, standing on one foot (gross motor skills) •Difficulty with writing, tying shoes (fine motor skills) **Stereotypic Movement Disorder (symptoms are repetitive and excessive)** •Head banging •Rocking back and forth •Hitting oneself •Biting oneself •Nail biting **Tourette's Disorder** •Simple tics involve brief/sudden repetitive movements – usually small movements •Complex tics involve larger complex movements •Vocal tics are random short words or sounds. **Persistent vocal or motor tic disorders include:** •Vocal sounds •Arm, leg or head jerking •Eye blinking •Unspecified tic •Other specified tic

Chapter 12

Neurocognitive Disorders: (previously known as Dementia)

Alzheimer's Disease
Delirium
Huntington's Disease
Parkinson's Disease

Conditions that lead to an individual's cognitive decline. These declines affect attention, memory, learning, perception, language, and social cognition.

Neurocognitive Disorders

Disorder	Overview
Delirium	**Significant deficit in cognition or memory compared to an individual's previous function.** **Risk groups:** Elderly, Burn victims, Drug users **Symptoms:** Inability to stay focused, Inability to articulate, Easily distracted, Withdrawn from activities **Cognitive:** Poor memory, Disorientation, Difficulty recalling words or speaking, Rambling speech, Difficulty understanding speech, Difficulty with reading or writing
Dementia	A general term for memory loss, language , thinking abilities, problem – solving that affect quality of life. Dementia covers a wide range of conditions that are grouped under "Dementia"
Alzheimer's Disease **A degenerative condition. No cure. Usually occurs after the age of 65.**	A **Stage 1:** 1-3 years Mild amnesia Diminished visuospatial skill Indifference Irritability Sadness Anomia **Stage 2:** 2-10 years Increased amnesia Restlessness Flat mood Delusions Aphasia Acalculia Inability to translate ideas (actions/movement) **Stage 3:** 8-12 years Severely impaired functioning Apathy Limb rigidity Fecal and urinary incontinence
Huntington's Disease	**A degenerative breakdown of cells in the brain. It is also an inherited disease. Appears between the ages of 30 and 40.** Symptoms vary amongst individuals. One individual may experience more movement disorder, versus another other who may experience more cognitive disorders. Irritability, Depression, Forgetfulness, Dementia, Fidgeting, Clumsiness Involuntary quick jerks
Parkinson's Disease	**A progressive disorder of the nervous system that affects movement.** Symptoms develop differently in people. Slow movement, Resting tremors, Loss of balance and/or coordination Violent restlessness, Depression, Dementia

Chapter 13

_____

Eating Disorders

Avoidant/Restrictive Food Intake Disorder
Anorexia Nervosa
Binge-Eating Disorder
Bulimia Nervosa
Rumination Disorder

Eating Disorders

Disorder	Overview
Bulimia Nervosa **Normal body weight**	**Is an overeating compulsion. Eating is characterized by episodes of binge eating followed be extreme efforts to avoid gaining weight. It is also persistent concern with body weight and shape.** **At least one episode per week for three months.** **Symptoms:** •Consuming amounts of food that are larger than most individuals would eat within the same time period •The individual feels a lack of control over eating •Eating alone and unexpected trips for food •Hiding of food **Binge eating followed by purging. Self-induced vomiting, laxatives, fasting; extreme exercise in order to prevent weight gain.**
Anorexia Nervosa **Low body weight**	**An obsessive worry about gaining too much weight. Individuals maintain/have significantly Low body weight**. Some individual restrict calories, exercise excessively, binge and/or purge, use laxatives, vomiting or diuretics to rid their calories **Symptoms include:** •Extreme restriction of food •Irrational fear of gaining weight •Irrational behaviors that prevent weight gain •Distorted body image •Insomnia •Fatigue •Hair thinning or falling out •Skin that is yellow or blotchy •Constipation •Dry skin •Low blood pressure •More than three missed periods
PICA	Persistent eating of non-food substances. Most common in children and pregnant women. **Symptoms must be present for at least one month. Additionally,** children will also eat regular food. •Paint •Pebbles •Hair •Sand

Eating Disorders

Disorder	Overview
Binge-Eating Disorder	At least one episode Binge eating followed by purging. Self-induced vomiting, laxatives, fasting; extreme exercise in order to prevent weight gain. **A persistent concern with body weight and shape.** Symptoms: •Eating rapidly than normal •Eating until full, uncomfortable •Eating food without feeling hungry •Eating aloe of embarrassment •Feeling of disgust with oneself
Avoidant/Restrictive Food Intake Disorder	The individual consumes only certain foods (also know as "picky eating"). The choice of food is based on texture, appearance, smell, taste, and prior previously bad experiences with certain foods. This often results in nutrition deficiencies. **Symptoms:** •Inadequate food intake (results in nutritional deficiencies) •Adults - weight loss. In children - failure to gain weight •Psychosocial decline •Supplements are used to maintain needed nutrients •Individual does not have distorted body image or medical condition
Rumination Disorder	Is an eating disorder, usually an infant or young child, re-chews partially digested good that has been swallowed. This is isn't an involuntarily or or forced as in vomiting. Many times the re-chewed food is swallowed and at times the food may be spit out. Regurgitation occurs between a half hour to two hours after a meal. Regurgitation of food for at least a month **Symptoms:** •Repeated regurgitation of food •Repeated re-chewing of food •Repeated indigestion and stomach aches •Chapped/raw lips •Weight loss •Tooth decay and bad breath

Chapter 14

Substance Abuse Disorders

Alcohol Intoxication and Withdrawal
Amphetamine and Cocaine Intoxication and Withdrawal
Nicotine Addiction and Withdrawal

Substance Abuse Disorders

Disorder	Overview
Amphetamine and Cocaine Intoxication and Withdrawal	Amphetamine and cocaine are two different drugs that vary in effect. Cocaine **(illegal)** stimulates the central nervous system, causing a feeling of euphoria. Amphetamine also induces euphoria, but is a **legal** drug used for those with ADHD, narcolepsy, and severe cases of fatigue. **Symptoms of intoxication:** •Seizures •Confusion •Muscle weakness •Nausea and/or vomiting •Weight loss •Agitation •Dilated pupils •Hypertension •Psychological changes/ maladaptive behavior (sexual/ aggressive behavior, impaired judgment, paranoid ideation, auditory hallucinations, euphoria, anger) **Withdrawal symptoms:** •Fatigue •Unpleasant dreams •Insomnia and/or hypersomnia •Increase in appetite •Severe depression •Retardation and/or psychomotor agitation .

Substance Abuse Disorders

Disorder	Overview
Nicotine Addiction and Withdrawal	Individual is dependent on nicotine. The effects of nicotine include: enhanced memory, improved concentration, appetite suppression, respiration increase, and hypertension. **Withdrawal symptoms:** •Inability to concentrate •Inability to focus •Anxiety •Weight gain •Agitation •Depression
Alcohol Intoxication and Withdrawal	**Symptoms of intoxication:** •Slurred speech •Poor coordination •Uncontrolled eye movements •Impairment of memory and/or attention •Psychological changes/ maladaptive behavior (sexual/aggressive behavior, impaired judgment) •Coma •Gait is affected **Withdrawal symptoms:** •Hand tremors •Insomnia •Vomiting and/or nausea •Anxiety •Agitation, psychomotor •Long use can cause seizures •Hallucinations/illusions **Withdrawal delirium:** •Hallucinations •Delusions •Agitation •Cognitive disturbances

Chapter 15

Sleep-wake Disorders

Breathing-Related
Insomnia
Circadian Rhythm Sleep-Wake
Hypersomnolence
Non-Rapid Eye Movement Disorder
Narcolepsy
Rapid Eye Movement Disorder

Sleep-Wake Disorders

Disorder	Overview
Insomnia	When an individual has difficulty falling asleep and/or staying asleep. Starts in young adulthood. •Must occur at least three nights a week •Must occur for at least three months •Must cause significant distress in functioning **Variations:** **Episodic** - lasts under three months **Persistent** - lasts longer than three months **Recurrent** - several episodes in a year
Circadian Rhythm Sleep-Wake	An individual's inability to go to sleep and wake up on time for social needs, work, and school. **Symptoms:** •Individual fails to fall asleep until late at night and results in oversleeping
Non-Rapid Eye Movement Disorder	Individual's brain is partially awake and partly in REM sleep. **Experiences** •Sleep walking •Sleep terrors •Sleep sex During sleep time, the individual can perform actions without being aware.
Rapid Eye Movement Disorder	An individual will awaken from REM sleep and act out their dreams: shouting, hitting, punching, and getting out of bed.

Sleep-Wake Disorders

Disorder	Overview
Breathing-Related	When an individual's breathing is interrupted during sleep; snoring. There are three types: **Obstructive Sleep Apnea** •The individual's upper airway closes, partly or fully, but breathing continues **Central Sleep Apnea** •The individual's respiration ceases because of a decrease in ventilatory drive **Mixed Sleep Apnea** •The individual shows signs of both OSA and CSA
Hypersomnolence	Excessive sleep in the daytime or at night. Individual often naps during the day. **Symptoms** – occurs at least three times a week for at least one month (acute condition) or three months (persistent) •Causes distress in function (social, occupational) •Not associated due to another disorder, medical reason, medication, or drugs
Narcolepsy	Individual experiences sleep during the day and attacks of sudden sleep during the day. **Symptoms:** •Hallucinations •Excessive daytime sleep •Loss of muscle tone and muscle control •Inability to move or speak
Nightmare Disorder	An individual experiences nightmares, which often cause distress. The disturbing nightmares prevent an individual from getting enough sleep.

Chapter 16

Sexual Dysfunctions

Delayed Ejaculation
Erectile Disorder
Female Orgasmic Disorder
Female Sexual Interest/Arousal Disorder
Genito-Pelvic Pain/Penetration Disorder
Male Hypoactive Sexual Desire Disorder
Premature Ejaculation

Delayed/Premature Ejaculation	Erectile Disorder	Male Hypoactive Sexual Desire Disorder
Delayed - Also known as impaired ejaculation. Symptoms must be present for at least three months: •Prolonged period of sexual stimulation for a man to ejaculate •Can occur in all sexual situations or with certain partners (situational delayed ejaculation) •Symptoms cause stress for the individual •Condition is not caused by another medical condition Premature – **when ejaculation occurs sooner than a man and partner would like during sex.** **Symptoms:** •Conditions are present for at least six months •Ejaculation occurs in under a minute •Condition causes frustration, stress, and tension between partners •Symptoms cause stress for the individual •Condition must not be caused by a medical condition	The inability for a man to get and or keep an erection firm enough for sex. Symptoms are present for at least six months. One or more symptoms must be present. **Symptoms:** •Unable to get an erection •Unable to maintain an erection during sex Symptoms can be situational or occur all the time.	A lack of sexual fantasies and/or desire for sexual activity. Symptoms present for at least six months: •Low sexual desire over 50% of the time •Delay or absence of orgasm during sex •Ejaculates within under a minute •Causes stress to the individual

Female Orgasmic Disorder	Female Sexual Interest/Arousal Disorder	Female Genito-Pelvic Pain Disorder
When an individual has difficulty reaching orgasm. Symptoms must be present for six months and not be explained by a medical condition: •Includes unsatisfying orgasm •Taking long to climax •Can occur during sex or masturbation •Causes distress	The inability or persistent ability for a women to either achieve or maintain sexual arousal. Three or more symptoms must be present for at least six months: •Lack of interest in sexual activity •Absence of thoughts of sexual activity •Lack of initiating sexual encounters •Lack of pleasure during sex •Causes distress for women •Not caused by a medical condition	The difficulty of having sex because of significant pain during intercourse. Symptoms must be present for six months. One or more symptoms must be present: •Pain in the genital/pelvic area during sex causes tightening •Fear of sex because of the anticipated pain •Tightening of the pelvis when attempting intercourse •Avoiding sex

Chapter 17

Paraphilic Disorders

Exhibitionistic
Fetishistic
Frotteuristic
Transvestic
Pedophilic Disorder
Sexual Masochism Disorder
Sexual Sadism Disorder
Voyeuristic

Transvestic	These fantasies or behaviors must be present for at least six months and cause severe distress (dysfunction in social settings or other areas of daily life). Recurrent and intense sexual arousal from cross dressing.
Frotteuristic	These acts are more often seen in males between the ages of 15 and 25. These acts continue for more than six months. The disorder involves intense fantasies, sexual arousal, urges that are centered on the act of touching/rubbing on non-consenting people. These behaviors are repetitive and usually occur in crowded places.
Exhibitionistic	The individual has recurrent urges over a period of six months. This disorder is marked by an individual's urge or fantasy of exposing one's genitals to unsuspecting people.
Voyeuristic	The individual must experience the disorder for at least six months and must be at least 18 yrs old. This disorder is marked by an individual's arousal from a fantasy or act of watching unsuspecting people who are naked, or partially clothed. The individual is not interested in having sex with the individuals being observed.
Fetishistic	The individual must experience the fetish arousal for at least six months. The fantasies cause significant distress or affect occupation and personal functioning. This disorder is characterized as an intense sexual arousal from the use of an inanimate object that causes distress or impairment. This disorder interferes with normal sexual functioning and arousal is impossible without the fetish object (high heels or other shoes, leather clothing, undergarments, toes, hair, feet). Sexual gratification can only be obtained with the fetish.

Sexual Masochism Disorder	Sexual Sadism Disorder
Recurrent sexual fantasies, urges, and behavior that cause severe harm to self and/or others. Symptoms are present for at least six months and must be real acts, not fantasies. Sexual acts include asphyxiophilia, suffering, or humiliation. •Causes distress in areas of functioning - social/occupational •Beaten •Bound •Other ways an individual can suffer	Constant fantasies in which sexual excitement results from inflicting physical or psychological suffering on a partner. These acts are seen as power over the victim. Will never seek treatment on their own. Can include: •Humiliation •Terror •Rape •Torture •Murder

Pedophilic Disorder
Intense sexual arousal with fantasies or behaviors involving prepubescent adolescents (usually under the age of 13). Urges are present for six months. **Symptoms:** •Intense sexual fantasies •Urges or behaviors involving sexual activity with a prepubescent •Sexual urges have been acted on •The individual is at least 16 years old and 5 years older than the prepubescent

Chapter 18

Gender Dysphoria

Gender Dysphoria

Appears in children (2 yrs) through adulthood

The individual strongly identifies with the opposite gender.

Symptoms in Children – must be present for six months:
•Incongruence with their own gender
•Strong desire to be the other gender
•Crossdressing (boys)
•Wears masculine clothing (girls)
•During play the child will have preference to role play the opposite gender
•During play the child chooses toys intended for the opposite gender
•Uncomfortable with their own anatomy
•Children are distressed in areas of relationships

Symptoms in Adolescents and Adults:
•Incongruence with their expressed gender, sexual organs, and characteristics (the incongruence is present for at least six months)
•The desire to have the sex characteristics of the other gender
•The desire to be the other gender, includes wanting to be treated like the other gender and wanting to think like the other gender.
•Excessive stress in relationships, family, friends, and social settings

Chapter 21

Bonus Information

How to break down a disorder
What is a provisional/plausible diagnosis
What is a rule out
What is a differential diagnosis

How to break down a disorder

Easy steps to help you recognize the difference and similarities in disorders so you can diagnose a patient

Ask.........................

1. Why is the client seeking therapy?
2. What are the clients symptoms?
3. How long has the client been had these symptoms?
4. Is the client on medication?
5. Has the client experienced trauma?
6. Has the client ever been hospitalized?
7. Has the client been in therapy? How long ago? Clients diagnosis?

Use this table to help you diagnosis

Presenting Problem	Symptoms	Duration	Rule Out	Diagnosis & Treatment

On the next page you will find a case example showing how the table is used.

> **Sample Case**
>
> Mary is a 15-year-old popular high school student, who is tall, slender, and maintains her weight at 98 pounds; she's a picky eater to stay fit for sports.
>
> She has been experiencing crying episodes, sporadically, for several months. During these episodes, she tells her mother that she has stomachaches, headaches, feels tired and, at times, can't concentrate. Additionally, she hasn't been sleeping well and finds herself getting up every morning at 5:30 to prepare for the day.
>
> Mary does well in school, but often worries about her grades. She has many friends and is well-liked. Lately, however, she has been feeling out of place with her friends, and this worries her. Being part of the popular group is important to her, and if her friends were to drop her from the group, she'd be devastated. She is part of the swim team and captain of her cheerleading squad. Mary tells you that she's been stressed for seven months and doesn't know how to control what she's feeling.

Mary	Symptoms	Duration	Diagnosis
Presenting Problem Feels stressed Can't concentrate	Irritable Can't sleep Fatigue Stomachaches	Seven months	Generalized Anxiety Disorder

Generalized Anxiety Disorder

The individual has excessive worry about events or activities, such as money, family, or work.

This anxiety must exist for at least **six months** and must be difficult to control. The anxiety is also disproportionate to the fear.

Anxiety must include three of the following:

1. Sleep disturbance
2. Irritability
3. Difficulty concentrating
4. Muscle tension
5. Exertion or fatigue
6. Restlessness
7. Chronic headaches

The next several pages contain cases so you can formulate your diagnosis

Practice

Bill is a 49-year-old man who comes to see you after his girlfriend of four years left him, seven weeks ago. His previous relationship lasted for two years. He's unable to sleep through the night, feels sad, and has occasional body aches – symptoms that lasted four months after the first break-up. He relays that lately his job has been stressful and he's finding it difficult to concentrate. Once a social person, he now feels withdrawn. He shares that he hurt his ankle two weeks ago and is unable to exercise, adding to his misery and making him anxious. He says he has no thoughts of suicide and wants to feel better.

Presenting Problem	Symptoms	Duration	Rule Out	Diagnosis

Practice

Craig is a 24-year-old man. He was a mechanic in the army for six years, whose job was to assure the safety and reliability of Army vehicles. He was last stationed in the Middle East, and decided not to go back to the Army after he returned from tour. Craig has been home for twelve months, and lives with his parents. He has been dating Sara for the last eight months. Craig works as a mechanic at a nearby shop in his hometown. He works long days at the shop, because for the last nine months he has been going to work late. Craig has been unable to sleep, is easily startled, and is having a hard time remembering things. He's also having nightmares. Sara is worried about Craig, and calls you for help.

Presenting Problem	Symptoms	Duration	Rule Out	Diagnosis

Practice

Liza is a 41-year-old waitress who works in a very hip bar in the city. Liza has a ten-year-old daughter and seven-year-old son. Liza's husband, Steve, left her eight years ago. Steve finally left Liza because he could not handle her neediness and privative ways.

Liza needs constant attention and dresses very provocatively. Her employer has to regularly remind her to dress a little more conservatively, as her co-workers are bothered by the way she dresses. Liza looks for attention, and when she doesn't get the attention she needs, she can become very moody. Liza is always looking to pick up the "right" customer. She wants a man who will cherish her. Liza has dated many customers from the bar, and many stay away from her because they know she makes up stories about how in love a man is with her. Liza is also manipulative and shallow, and has a tendency to exaggerate. Her employer has become concerned with her and recommends that she seek therapy. Liza thinks he's crazy, but is willing to go because she needs this job.

Presenting Problem		Symptoms		Duration		Rule Out		Diagnosis

Practice

Patty is a four-year-old girl who has been experiencing anxiety when she is around groups of kids. Patty's mom, Joyce, has spoken to her preschool teacher and has tried to come with ways to help Patty. Patty will sit alone in school while other kids try to communicate with her and include her in activities. Patty listens and follows directions from her teachers, and will speak to them when she needs something, but she won't speak to the kids in class. Claire has taken Patty to the doctor and found that Patty is in good health. Patty's pediatrician refers you to a therapist.

Presenting Problem	Symptoms	Duration	Rule Out	Diagnosis

Practice

Fran is a tall, slender, popular 15-year-old high school student, who maintains her weight at 98 pounds. She's a picky eater to stay fit for sports.

She has been experiencing crying episodes, sporadically, for several months. During these episodes, she tells her mother that she has stomachaches, headaches, feels tired and, at times, can't concentrate. Additionally, she hasn't been sleeping well and finds herself getting up every morning at 5:30 to prepare for the day.

Fran does well in school, but often worries about her grades. She has many friends and is well-liked. Lately, however, she has been feeling out of place with her friends, and this worries her. Being part of the popular group is important to her, and if her friends were to drop her from the group, she'd be devastated. She is part of the swim team and captain of her cheerleading squad. Fran tells you that she's been stressed for seven months and doesn't know how to control what she's feeling.

| Presenting Problem | Symptoms | Duration | Rule Out | Diagnosis |

Practice

Cody is a 26-year-old computer programmer at a small company in his hometown. Cody lives with his girlfriend, Carrie. Carrie moved in with Cody two months ago, and is starting to wonder if it was the right choice. Carrie is overwhelmed by Cody's behavior. Last weekend, Cody spent 15 hours watching TV, detailed his car and brainstormed on how to start his own business. During this time, he flew from idea to idea and could barely keep up with his rapid speech. He was convinced that he could make a million dollars if he had his own company. Then, four days later, Cody lost interest in his ideas, was exhausted, and felt hopeless. Carrie noticed his behavior change from feeling that he could do anything (although he took no action on these ideas), to being depressed. These moods last from four days of being on top of the world, to a week of being down. More often, Cody experiences emptiness and sadness, but not often or severe enough to affect his job or social life. Carrie doesn't know how to help Cody and tells him she wants to attend therapy.

Presenting Problem	Symptoms	Duration	Rule Out	Diagnosis

Practice

John is a six-year-old boy who is coming into therapy at the request of his mother, Gail. When John and Gail meet with you, you notice that John won't sit still. He is rude to his mother by interrupting her, and won't sit down. John's mother asks him to sit down and behave, and he shouts back at her, "No." Gail tells you that she can't handle John and needs help. She informs you that John's aggressive and destructive behavior has been going on for over the last three years. John has been suspended from school, has broken items at home, abuses the family cat, and hits his sister.

Presenting Problem	Symptoms	Duration	Rule Out	Diagnosis

Key Words to Know

In this section you will learn about differential diagnosis, plausible diagnosis and rule out.

It can be confusing, but you'll get it!. Remember keep it simple, stay focused and pay attention to key words to help you learn.

Key Words to Know

Provisional/Plausible Diagnosis	A therapist is not certain of a diagnosis because more information is needed. **Preliminary diagnosis is an "educated guess" based on an information provided by the client. Once more information is gathered, an accurate diagnosis is made.**

Example:

Margo is stressed over her fears that her boyfriend will break up with her. Margo has been picking her skin and hiding the scars from him and her friends by covering them with long shirts. What is the provisional/plausible diagnosis:

> Obsessive Compulsive Disorder
> Body Dysmorphia Disorder

Rule Out	**Attempting to determine whether a client meets the criteria for a specific diagnosis** • Good faith is needed from client. If client is not honest or does not provide all symptoms, it makes it difficult to properly diagnose • Attempt to pinpoint the primary disorder based on the common presenting problems • What are the differences between the disorders? • Is substance abuse a factor? Are symptoms due to substance abuse? • Are symptoms related to a general medical condition?

Example:

Jim is always late or calling in sick for work. He states that his body aches and stomach issues are so severe that he has a hard time getting out of bed. Jim is exercising regularly to stay healthy. Jim's boss is concerned and recommends he sees a therapist.

Based on the information provided, what disorder would you rule out?

Malingering Disorder
Factious Disorder
Obsessive Compulsive Disorder
Social Anxiety Disorder

Key Words to Know

Differential Diagnosis	Attempting to determine if the diagnosis chosen is the correct diagnosis or if the diagnosis has some **overlap with other diagnoses.**
	• More than one possible diagnosis is present • The symptoms are shared with other disorders • Therapist will differentiate between the other diagnosis to determine the correct diagnosis • Based on symptoms/including medical history • Rule out other disorders • A result of drug-related conditions • Triggered by a specific event or situation • A result of stress

Differential Diagnosis of Bipolar I Disorder

More than one possibility exists

* You are removing diagnoses based on common symptoms *

Symptoms similar to Bipolar I Disorder

- Major Depressive Disorder
  - Can have hypomanic or manic symptoms
- ADHD
  - Distractibility and mood-related symptoms are similar to manic episodes
- Bipolar II Disorder
  - Individual can never have a full manic episode
- Personality Disorders
  - Borderline Personality Disorder has many symptoms that overlap with Bipolar I

Chapter 20

Bonus Section

The next several pages contain common disorders that many individuals have a difficult time differentiating. The format may help you better understand the disorder.

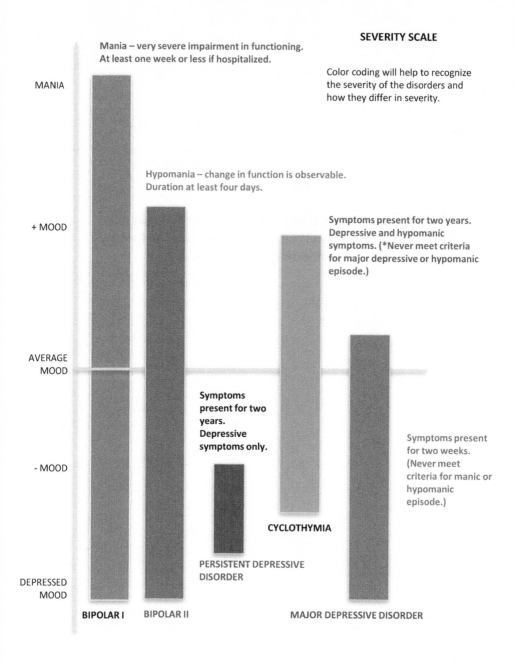

SEVERITY SCALE

Mania – very severe impairment in functioning.
At least one week or less if hospitalized.

Color coding will help to recognize
the severity of the disorders and
how they differ in severity.

MANIA

Hypomania – change in function is observable.
Duration at least four days.

+ MOOD

Symptoms present for two years.
Depressive and hypomanic
symptoms. (*Never meet criteria
for major depressive or hypomanic
episode.)

AVERAGE
MOOD

**Symptoms
present for two
years.
Depressive
symptoms only.**

Symptoms present
for two weeks.
(Never meet
criteria for manic or
hypomanic
episode.)

- MOOD

CYCLOTHYMIA

PERSISTENT DEPRESSIVE
DISORDER

DEPRESSED
MOOD

BIPOLAR I   BIPOLAR II   MAJOR DEPRESSIVE DISORDER

Example of what creativity looks like for individuals who are and are not bipolar

Somewhat stuck		
Not motivated		
Slow to complete tasks		**Bipolar individual:**
Too cautious	**Most people are here:**	Over the top
Can be boring	Not too spontaneous	Risk taking
Not a risk taker	Will explore new ideas	Over talkative
	Enjoys routine	Racing thoughts
	Can be more outgoing but never to the extreme	Poor judgment
	Basically "comfortable" and not affecting quality of life in a negative way	Flood of ideas that tend to be damaging
		Hallucinates

Full mania

0-30	40 - 89	90-100
		EXTREME

Scale 0 - 100

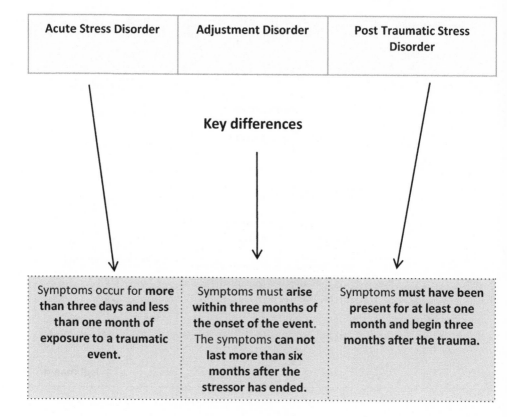

Acute Stress Disorder	Adjustment Disorder	Post Traumatic Stress Disorder

Key differences

Symptoms occur for **more than three days and less than one month of exposure to a traumatic event.**	Symptoms must **arise within three months of** the onset of the event. The symptoms **can not last more than six months after the stressor has ended.**	Symptoms **must have been present for at least one month and begin three months after the trauma.**

5 of the 8 symptoms must be present

- Excessive social anxiety
- Ideas of reference
- Odd beliefs/magical thinking
- Lacks close friends (excluding family)
- Bodily illusions
- Suspiciousness/paranoid ideation
- Inappropriate/constricted affect
- Peculiarities in appearance or behavior

Schizotypal Personality Disorder

Schizoid Personality Disorder

4 of the 6 symptoms must be present

Including:
Pervasive lack of interest in relationships and limited emotional expression with others (coldness, detachment, or flattened affectivity)

- Lacks close friends (excluding family)
- Detachment or emotional coldness
- Takes pleasure in few activities
- Little interest in sexual relationships
- Almost always chooses solitary activities
- Indifferent to praise/criticism

4 of these symptoms must be present

Avoidant Personality Disorder

- Fears social risks
- Avoids social situations
- Difficult to meet people
- Low self-esteem
- They are shy, timid, and inhibited (socially)
- They want relationships, but find it difficult to have them

They are HYPERSENSITIVE to rejection and negative feedback.

They feel inadequate, incapable, undesirable

Schizotypal = schizoid symptoms + odd behavior and magical thinking Individuals with this disorder have difficulties forming and maintaining relationships

Mild

Schizotypal Personality Disorder

Schizophreniform Disorder

The individual experiences psychotic symptoms due to extreme trauma, stress, assault, or death of a loved one

An individual who experiences psychosis (cannot tell the difference between real and imagined).This disorder is on the schizophrenia spectrum and needs two major symptoms for diagnosis.

Brief Psychotic Disorder

SEVERE

Schizophrenia

Schizoaffective Disorder

An individual who experiences psychosis (cannot tell the difference between real and imagined) is unable to express emotion or relate to others. Symptoms are described as either positive or negative.

- Chronic and severe
- Affects an individual's way of thinking, emotions, and behavior.

Chronic and condition is characterized primarily by symptoms of **schizophrenia** and symptoms of **MOOD Disorder**

An individual who experiences persistent psychotic symptoms (schizophrenia symptoms) and major mood disorder (depression or bipolar disorder).

Borderline Personality Disorder

Impulsive

Reckless

Unstable relationships

Brief psychotic mood swings

Inflated sense of self-worth

Lacks empathy

Arrogant

Envious

Exploits others

Narcissistic Personality Disorder

Vulnerable

Needs constant praise

Seductive

Manipulative

Flirtatious

Histrionic Personality Disorder

Obsessive Compulsive Personality Disorder

Is
OBSESSED WITH

INEFFICIENT

- ➢ Schedules
- ➢ Details
- ➢ Rules
- ➢ Perfectionism
- ➢ Orderliness
- ➢ Complete Control

➢ Spends extra time with planning and worrying

ALSO inflexible, easily stressed, and tends to be rigid in beliefs and moral issues

Obsessive Compulsive Disorder		Obsessive Personality Disorder	
EGO – DYSTONIC – wishes they could stop	⬅ **Key Difference**	EGO – SYNTONIC – happy with how they are, don't want to change ➤	
Obsessions	**Compulsions**	**Obsessions**	
Germs	Cleaning	Perfectionism	Inefficient
Feels unsafe	Checking	Control	•Spends too much
Bad things will	Repeating	Rules	time planning and/or
happen	Arranging	Details	worrying
Discord		Schedules	•Very rigid with moral
		Orderliness	issues and beliefs
			•Is perceived as
			stubborn

Adjustment Disorders

Adjustment Disorders
Anxiety Disorder
Binge Eating Disorder
Bipolar Disorder
Gender Dysphoria
Histrionic Personality Disorder
Narcissistic Personality Disorder
Obsessive Compulsive Disorder
Panic Disorder
PTSD
Postpartum Disorder
Seasonal Affective Disorder
Rett's Disorder
Separation Anxiety Disorder
Sleepwalking Disorder

Anxiety Disorders

Acute Stress Disorder
Adjustment Disorder
Agoraphobia
Alzheimer's
Antisocial Personality Disorder
Anxiety Disorder
Borderline Personality
Dependent Personality
Generalized Anxiety
Hypochondriasis
Intermittent Explosive
Narcolepsy
Obsessive Compulsive
Obsessive Compulsive Personality
Panic Disorder
Paranoid Personality
PTSD
Selective Mutism
Separation anxiety
Sexual Dysfunction
Social Anxiety

Cognitive Disorders

Alzheimer's Disease
Attention Deficit Hyperactivity Disorder
Breathing Related Sleep Disorder
Dissociative Amnesia
Dissociative Disorder
Learning Disorders
Parkinson's Disease

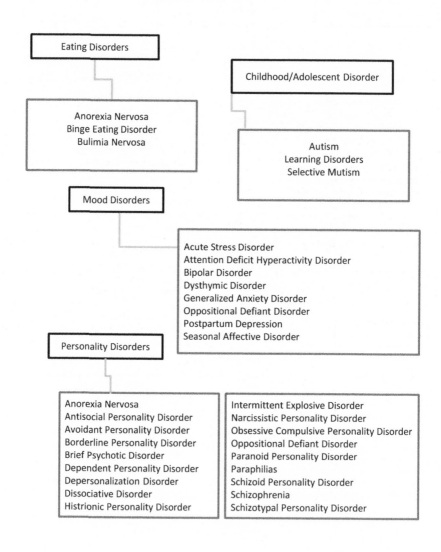

References

American Psychiatric Association, Diagnostic and Statistical Manual for Mental Disorders, DSM-5 (2013) APA Press; 5th Edition

Corcoran & Fisher, (2000). *Measures for Clinical Pr*actice: A Sourcebook. 3rd Edition. Free Press

Corcoran & Fisher, (2007). *Measures for Clinical Practice and Research*: A Sourcebook. NY, NY; Oxford University Press

Corey, G (2017). *Theory and Practice of Counseling and Psychotherapy*. Boston, MA: Cengage Learning

Curran, L. A. (2013). *101 trauma-informed interventions: Activities, exercises and assignments for moving the client and therapy forward*. Eau Claire, WI: PESI

Drummond, R. Jones, K. (2009). *Assessment Procedures for Counselors and Helping Professionals*, 7th Edition. Prentice Hall

Gabbard, G.O., (2014). *Treatments of Psychiatric Disorders*, 3rd Edition, vol. 1 & 2. Washington, DC. American Psychiatric Press

Groth-Marnat, G. (1997). *Handbook of psychological assessment*. New York: Wiley

Johnston, D. W., & Johnston, M. (2001). *Comprehensive clinical psychology*. Amsterdam: Elsevier

Kress, V.E., & Paylo, M.J. (2014), *Treating those with mental disorders; A comprehensive approach to case conceptualization and treatment.* New York, NY:Pearson

Neukrug, E., & Fawcett, R.C. (2015). *Essentials of Testing and Assessment*: A practical guide to counselors, social workers, and psychologists. Stamford, CT: Cengage Learning

Reichenberg, Lourie W., & Seligman, Linda. (2016). *Selecting Effective Treatments*. A comprehensive Systematic Guide to Treating Mental Disorders, Hoboken, NJ:Wiley

Rosenthal, H. (2006). *Therapy's best:* Practical advice and gems of wisdom from twenty accomplished counselors and therapists. New York: Haworth Press

Rosenthal, H. (2017). *Encyclopedia of Counseling;* Master Review and Tutorial for the National Counselor Examination…., State Counseling Exam, and the Counselor Pepar. Place of Publication not Identified: Taylor & Francis

Roth, A., Fonagy, P., (2005), *What Works for Whom?* Second Edition; A Critical Review of Psychotherapy Research, NY:Guilford Press

Sammons, M & Schmidt, N. (eds.) (2001). *Combined Treatments for Mental Disorders,* Washington D.C.: American Psychological Press